·My·First·
Dictionary

Library of Congress Cataloging-in-Publication Data

Snow, Alan.
    My first dictionary / illustrated by Alan Snow.
       p.   cm.
    Summary: Gives a brief overview of the origin of words and defines
more than 300 words with labeled illustrations and a brief sentence.
    ISBN 0-8167-2515-2 (lib. bdg.)   ISBN 0-8167-2516-0 (pbk.)
    1. Picture dictionaries, English—Juvenile literature.   2. English
language—Dictionaries, Juvenile. [1. Picture dictionaries.]
I. Title.
PE1629.S6 1992
423. '1—dc20   91-23485

·My·First·
Dictionary

Illustrated by
Alan
Snow

Troll Associates

How Words Came to Be

About two million years ago, human beings used their tongues to help them eat and to make crude sounds. Grunts, hoots, cries, and howls were some of the sounds they made. All were fairly easy to understand.

But humans soon discovered that those sounds were not enough. They wanted to have their thoughts and ideas understood as well. And so, after many years, they developed other sounds with their tongues. Those sounds led to speech, a language of real words. The word *language* itself means "tongue."

Written language appeared thousands of years after spoken language. The oldest example of written language found on earth is word-pictures. They were made about 5,500 years ago in Asia.

Nearly every time people come together today, language is used. There are about 3,000 languages in the world right now. Chinese is the language spoken by the most people—about 750 million. Next comes English, spoken by more than 300 million people.

Of all human inventions, language ranks near the top in importance. Just imagine a world without it!

How to Use This Dictionary

My First Dictionary will help you learn and remember over 300 basic words. All these main words are listed in **dark** print. They are then used in sentences that will tell you what the words mean. In a few instances, a sample sentence, printed in *italics,* is also given. It will help you better understand how the word is used.

Almost every one of the basic words here has a picture with it. This picture will give you an even clearer idea of what the word means.

Looking up a word is as easy as A-B-C. Just flip the pages to the one that has the first letter of your word at the top. It will appear in a box. Then look down the list of words starting with that letter until you come to your word. If the word is **lion**, for example, turn to the first page where the **l** words appear. Then look down for the **li** words, and finally the **lio** words. Only one word in this dictionary begins with **lio**—**lion**. You've found it!

At the back of *My First Dictionary* are picture games, a secret message, a matching contest, and other fun things to do with words. They will show you just how exciting your new "word power" can be!

Aa

above

If something is **above** you, it is higher than you are.

across

When you go **across** something, you go from one side to the other.

address

Your **address** is where you live. Your street, town, state, zip code, and country make up your **address**.

airplane

An **airplane** is a machine that flies in the air. **Airplanes** have wings and engines.

alphabet

An **alphabet** is a list of all the letters that make words, put in a special order.

angry

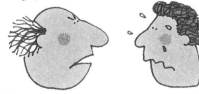

If you are **angry**, you are mad at someone or something.

animal

An **animal** is any living thing except a plant. People, dogs, fish, flies, and snails are all **animals**.

answer

If someone asks you a question, what you say next is your **answer**.

apple

An **apple** is a round fruit that grows on a tree. **Apples** can have red, yellow, or green skin.

asleep

When you are **asleep**, you are resting. You don't know what is going on around you.

awake

When you are **awake**, you are not sleeping. Your eyes are open, and you notice things around you.

Bb

baby

A **baby** is a very young boy or girl.

bad

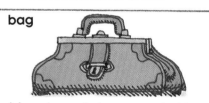

1. A **bad** person is someone who hurts others in some way.

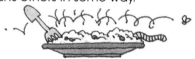

2. **Bad** food is not fit to eat.

bag

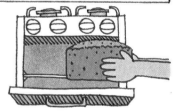

A **bag** is made to carry or hold things.

bake

When people **bake** food, they cook it in an oven.

ball

A **ball** is an object used in lots of games. **Balls** are usually round.

balloon

A **balloon** is a rubber bag filled with air or gas that makes it float.

Bb

bark

1. The **bark** of a tree is its skin.

2. The loud noise that a dog makes is its **bark**.

bat

1. A **bat** is a strong, often wooden, stick used in some games.

2. A **bat** is also a small, furry animal, like a mouse with wings. **Bats** fly mostly at night.

bath

When you sit in a bathtub and wash your whole body, you are taking a **bath**.

beach

The **beach** is the land along the edge of the ocean. It usually has sand or small stones on it.

bean

A **bean** is a flat, smooth seed or pod eaten as a vegetable.

bear

A **bear** is an animal that has thick fur and strong claws. It can stand on two feet.

bed

A **bed** is something to lie on when you rest or sleep.

bee

A **bee** is a flying insect. **Bees** make honey and wax.

below

If something is **below** you, it is lower than you are.

bicycle

A **bicycle** has two wheels. You can ride it by sitting on it and turning the pedals with your feet.

big

If something is **big**, it is great in size or amount.

bird

A **bird** is an animal with wings and feathers. Most **birds** can fly. Baby **birds** come from eggs.

birthday

Your **birthday** is a special day that you remember every year, because it was the day that you were born.

boat

A **boat** is something that can carry people, animals, and things on water.

body

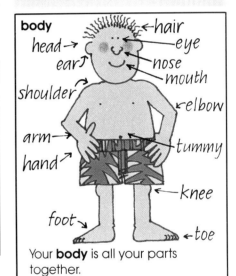

head → hair
ear → eye
nose
mouth
shoulder → elbow
arm → tummy
hand →
knee
foot → toe

Your **body** is all your parts together.

book

A **book** is made of pieces of paper attached together. **Books** often tell a story.

bottle

A **bottle** is usually made of glass or plastic. It is for holding things that you can pour, such as orange juice and cough syrup.

bottom

The **bottom** of something is its lowest part.

bowl

A **bowl** is a dish that's usually round and deep. It holds things such as food.

box

A **box** is a container that has straight sides and holds things such as toys. It often comes with a lid or top.

boy

A **boy** is a child who will be a man when he grows up.

brave

If you are **brave**, you can face pain or danger without fear.

bread

Bread is a food made with flour and baked in an oven.

break

If you **break** something, it falls apart, or stops working.

breakfast

Breakfast is the food you eat first thing in the morning.

bridge

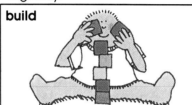

A **bridge** is a road that crosses above a river, a railroad, or a highway.

build

If you **build** something, you make it by putting things together.

bus

A **bus** is a machine that carries a lot of people along the road.

butterfly

A **butterfly** is an insect with four brightly colored wings.

buy

When you **buy** something, you get it by giving money for it.

can

1. If you say you **can** do something, that means you are able to do it.
2. A **can** is a container used to hold things or keep them fresh, such as food. **Cans** are often made of metal.

car

A **car** is a machine made to take a few people along roads.

carrot

A **carrot** is a vegetable. Its long, orange root grows underground.

carry

If you **carry** something, you lift it and take it with you.

cat

A **cat** is an animal that has short ears and usually has a long tail.

catch

If you **catch** something, you get hold of it while it is moving.

chair

A **chair** is something to sit on.

Cc

chase

If you **chase** somebody, you run after them to try to catch them.

cheese

Cheese is a food. It is made from milk.

chick

A **chick** is a young bird that has just come out of the egg.

circus

A **circus** is a place where you can see trained animals, acrobats, and clowns perform.

city

A **city** is a very large town. Many people live and work in **cities**.

clean

If something is **clean**, it has no dirt on it.

climb

If you **climb** something, such as a tree, you go up it, using your hands and feet.

clock

A **clock** is something that shows you what the time is.

clothes

hat
T-shirt
sweater
pants
underpants
socks
shoes

Your **clothes** are all the things that you wear to cover you and keep you warm.

cloud

Clouds are made up of tiny drops of water. They are gray or white and float high up in the sky.

cold

1. If the weather is **cold**, you need to wear a coat outside.

2. If you have a **cold**, you feel sick. **Colds** cause sneezing, coughing, and blocked or runny noses.

color

Red, blue, yellow, and green are all **colors**. There are a lot of different **colors**.

cook

When someone **cooks** food, they get it ready to eat by making it hot.

cookie

A **cookie** is a small, usually flat kind of cake that tastes sweet.

count

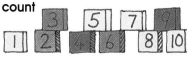

When you **count** things, you find out how many of them there are.

country

1. A **country** is the land where a nation of people lives. The United States is a **country**.

2. The **country** is land away from cities and most towns. There are trees and farms in the **country**.

cow

A **cow** is a big female farm animal that can give milk.

Cc

crawl

If you **crawl**, you move along on your hands and knees.

crayon

Crayons are colored wax sticks for drawing or writing.

cross

1. A **cross** is a shape made by two lines, sometimes like this.

2. If you **cross** something, such as a street, you go from one side to the other.

cup

A **cup** is something that you can drink from. Some **cups** have handles.

cut

1. If you **cut** yourself, it hurts and you bleed.

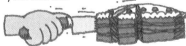

2. If you **cut** a cake, you make it into smaller pieces.

Dd

dance

When you **dance**, you move your whole body in a special way. People often **dance** to music.

dark

1. When it is **dark**, you cannot see very well because there is not enough light.

2. **Dark** hair is brown or black.

day

1. Your **day** is the time between getting up and going to bed.

2. A **day** is also part of a week. There are seven **days** in one week.

decide

When you **decide** to do something, you make up your mind about it.

deer

A **deer** is a very fast animal. Many **deer** have horns called antlers. **Deer** eat leaves and grass.

different

If two things are **different**, they are not like each other in one or more ways.

dig

When you **dig**, you turn over or make a hole in something such as earth or sand.

dinner

Dinner is the biggest or main meal of the day.

dirty

Something that is **dirty** is not clean.

dish

A **dish** is a plate or nearly flat bowl to put food on.

dive

If you **dive** into the water, you jump in headfirst.

dog

A **dog** is a four-legged animal that barks. There are many different kinds of **dogs**.

Dd

door

A **door** is a way into a house or a room. **Doors** open and close. Some **doors** swing, and some slide.

draw

When you **draw**, you make a pattern or a picture of something. You can **draw** with anything that will make a mark, such as a pencil, a pen, or a crayon.

dream

Dreams are pictures or ideas that happen in your mind when you are asleep.

dry

Something that is **dry** is not wet or damp.

duck

A **duck** is a bird that spends a lot of time in the water. **Ducks** have webbed feet so that they can swim well.

Ee

ear

Your **ear** is part of your body. You have one **ear** on each side of your head. You use your **ears** to hear sounds.

early

1. The **early** part of something is near the beginning of it. *They decided to get up early in the morning.*

2. If you get somewhere **early**, you are there before the time arranged. *They were a little early and had to wait for the show to start.*

earth

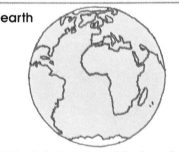

1. **Earth** is the planet that we live on. It is one of the nine planets that go around the sun.

2. **Earth** is also the ground that plants grow in.

eat

When you **eat**, you put food in your mouth. Then you chew it and swallow it.

egg

An **egg** is a round object laid by female birds and some insects, snakes, and fish. A baby animal grows in the **egg** until it is ready to be born.

elephant

An **elephant** is a very large, heavy animal. **Elephants** have big ears and a long nose called a trunk. An **elephant** can pick things up with its trunk.

empty

If something is **empty**, it has nothing in it.

explain

When you **explain** something, you talk about it so that people will understand.

eye

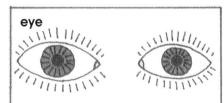

An **eye** is part of your body. Your **eyes** are in the front of your head. You see things with your **eyes**.

face

Your **face** is on the front of your head. Your eyes, nose, mouth, cheeks, and chin are all part of your **face**.

fair

1. A **fair** is a place where people can buy and sell things, and have fun.

2. Something that is **fair** seems right to most people.

fall

1. If you **fall**, you suddenly drop toward the ground.

2. **Fall** is the time of year between summer and winter. In the **fall**, leaves begin to **fall** from the trees.

farm

A **farm** is a piece of land that is used to grow food or to raise animals.

fast

People or things that are **fast** can move very quickly.

favorite

Your **favorite** is the one you like the most. *This is my **favorite** doll.*

feather

Feathers are the very light things that cover most of a bird's body.

feel

1. The way you **feel** is how you are at the time. You might **feel** happy, excited, or sad.

2. You **feel** something when you are touching it, or it is touching you. Fur can **feel** soft, sandpaper **feels** rough, and snow **feels** cold.

find

When you **find** something, you usually come upon the thing you were looking for.

fire

Fire is the hot flames that come from something burning.

fish

A **fish** is an animal that lives underwater. Most **fish** have fins. There are many different kinds of **fish**. Some are good to eat.

fit

If clothes **fit**, they are the right size for you. They are not too large or too small.

fix

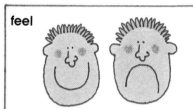

When people **fix** things, they make them work again.

float

When things **float**, they stay on top of the water or in the air.

floor

The **floor** of a room is the part that you walk on.

flower

A **flower** is part of a plant. **Flowers** are very pretty.

Ff

fly

1. Things that **fly** move through the air. Most birds can **fly**. If we want to **fly** somewhere, we usually go in an airplane.

2. A **fly** is a small insect with wings.

follow

When you **follow** somebody, you go after them.

food

Food is what we eat or drink. People, animals, and plants all need **food** to help them grow.

fork

A **fork** is something you use to eat food with. It is long and has two or more thin pointed parts on its end.

fox

A **fox** is a wild animal that looks something like a dog. It has a bushy tail and thick fur.

free

If something is **free**, you do not have to pay any money to get it.

friend

A **friend** is someone you like very much. A **friend** likes being with you, too.

frog

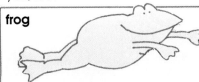

A **frog** is a small animal that spends a lot of time in the water. **Frogs** can jump a long way.

fruit

A **fruit** is the part of a plant that has seeds. Apples and grapes are **fruits** that can be eaten.

full

If something is **full**, it will not hold any more.

funny

Something that is **funny** makes you laugh.

fur

Fur is thick hair that grows on an animal's body. **Fur** keeps animals warm.

Gg

game

A **game** is something you play. Hide-and-seek is a **game**.

garden

A **garden** is a place where flowers or vegetables are grown. Many **gardens** are near people's homes.

girl

A **girl** is a child who will be a woman when she grows up.

good

1. A person who is **good** is kind and caring.

2. If you say a food or a show was **good**, you mean you enjoyed it.

grass

Grass is a green plant. It has thin leaves that grow closely together. You can see **grass** in lawns and in fields.

grow

When living things **grow**, they get larger.

Hh

hair

Hair is the thin growth on the bodies of people and some animals.

half

If you cut something in **half**, you cut it into two parts that are the same size.

happy

When you are **happy**, you feel very good. You are **happy** when something nice has happened or when things are the way you want them to be.

hard

1. If something is **hard**, it is firm and solid. Rocks are **hard**.

$$345123 \times 234 =$$

2. If you say something was **hard** to do, you mean you had to work at it or give it a lot of effort.

hat

A **hat** is something to wear on your head.

hear

When you **hear** something, sounds are coming into your ears.

heavy

Something that is **heavy** is hard to pick up.

help

When you **help** somebody, you do something for them.

hide

If you **hide** something, you put it where it can't be seen.

high

Something that is **high** in the air is a long way off the ground.

hill

A **hill** is land that is higher than the land around it.

hit

If you **hit** something, you strike it or come up against it hard.

hole

A **hole** is an opening or hollow place in something. *The dog was about to jump through the **hole** in the fence.*

horse

A **horse** is a four-legged animal that people can ride.

Hh

hot

1. If something is **hot**, it burns when you touch it.

2. If you feel **hot**, you are too warm.

hour

An **hour** is part of a day. There are twenty-four **hours** in one day.

house

A **house** is a building for people to live in.

hungry

When you are **hungry**, you want something to eat.

hurt

If you **hurt** part of your body, it feels pain.

Ii

ice

Frozen water is called **ice**. When water turns into **ice**, it becomes solid and you can't pour it.

idea

When people have an **idea**, they think of a way to do something.

important

Someone or something that is **important** matters a lot.

insect

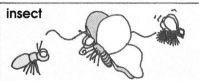

An **insect** is a very small animal with six legs. Most **insects** have wings. Ants and butterflies are **insects**.

inside

The **inside** of something is the part that has a covering around it.

invite

When you **invite** someone, you ask them to do something with you.

island

An **island** is a piece of land that has water all around it.

Jj

join

1. When you **join** two things, you fasten them together.

2. If you **join** a group, you become a member.

joke

A **joke** is something funny. People tell **jokes** or do things as a **joke** to make you laugh.

juice

Juice is a liquid. You can get **juice** from fruit, vegetables, and meat. You squeeze an orange and the **juice** comes out.

jump

When you **jump**, you throw yourself into the air.

Kk

key

A **key** is a small piece of metal that can open or close a lock. *Use the key to open the door.*

kick

You **kick** something by hitting it with your foot.

kiss

If you **kiss** somebody, you touch them with your lips.

kite

A **kite** is a light toy. You can fly a **kite** in the wind on the end of a string.

kitten

A **kitten** is a baby cat.

knife

A **knife** is something sharp that you can cut with.

knock

When you **knock** something, you hit it.

knot

A **knot** is the place where string or rope is tied.

Ll

ladder

Ladders are steps you can move from place to place. **Ladders** are used for climbing up or down things.

lake

A **lake** is a large body of water surrounded by land.

land

1. **Land** is the part of the earth that is not covered by the oceans. We live on the **land**.
2. When something **lands**, it comes to the ground from the air or water.

late

1. The **late** part of something is near the end of it. *They will be here late in the afternoon.*

2. If you are **late**, you get to a place after the time you were supposed to be there. *I was late for school today.*

lead

When you **lead**, you go in front of other people.

learn

When you **learn** something, you get to know it.

left

Everything has a **left** side and a right side. The **left** side of a page is the side that you begin reading on in English.

letter

1. A **letter** is a mark such as **A** or **C** that stands for a sound. You use **letters** to make words.

2. A **letter** is also a written message you send to somebody.

lick

If you **lick** something, you move your tongue over it.

lift

To **lift** something is to pick it up or raise it.

light

1. **Light** is a form of energy that lets us see. The sun, candles, and lamps all give off **light**.

2. Something that is **light** has little weight and is easy to lift.

Ll

like

If you **like** somebody or something, that person or thing makes you happy.

lion

A **lion** is a big, strong, wild cat.

lonely

If you feel **lonely**, you are unhappy because you are by yourself.

lose

If you **lose** something, you can't find it anywhere.

loud

Something that is **loud** makes a lot of noise.

love

If you **love** someone, you like them very much.

low

When something is **low**, it is close to the ground or below the usual level.

lunch

Lunch is a meal that you eat between breakfast and dinner.

Mm

magic

In stories, **magic** makes impossible things happen. Some people can do tricks, which look like **magic**. They can make things appear and disappear.

make

When you **make** something, you build it. *Shall we **make** a box out of paper?*

man

A **man** is an adult male person. A boy grows up to be a **man**.

meal

A **meal** is food that people eat at certain times of the day. Breakfast, lunch, and dinner are **meals**.

measure

You can **measure** something to find out how big or heavy it is. *Use your ruler to **measure** that piece of paper.*

meat

Meat is the parts of an animal that are used for food.

melt

When ice cubes **melt**, they change back into water.

milk

Milk is a white liquid food you can drink. The **milk** we drink usually comes from cows.

minute

A **minute** is part of an hour. There are sixty **minutes** in one hour.

mix

When you **mix** different things, you put them together. You **mix** flour, butter, sugar, and eggs to make a cake.

money

Money is something you use to buy things with.

monkey

A **monkey** is an animal that is very good at climbing trees. **Monkeys** have strong hands and feet to help them move through the tree branches.

Mm

month

A **month** is part of a year. There are twelve **months** in one year.

moon

The **moon** is the pale yellow or white ball you can see in the sky at night. The **moon** moves from west to east around the earth.

mountain

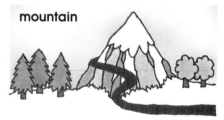

A **mountain** is land that is a lot higher than the land around it.

mouse

A **mouse** is a furry animal with a long, thin tail.

mouth

Your **mouth** is the place you put food into when you eat. You also use your **mouth** to make words and sounds.

music

Music is made up of special sounds that are nice to hear. The sounds are made by singing or such things as a guitar.

Nn

name

A **name** is a word that you call somebody or something. *Our new baby's name is Joe.*

near

If something is **near** you, it is not very far away.

nest

A **nest** is a home that some animals make for their babies.

new

When something is **new**, it has not been used before.

nice

Something **nice** is something that you like.

night

Night is the time when it is dark outside.

nose

Your **nose** is the part that sticks out of the middle of your face. You use your **nose** for smelling and breathing.

number

A **number** is a symbol or word that can tell you how many things there are. *The **number** of fingers here is five.*

Oo

ocean

An **ocean** is a very, very large area of water. Fish and other animals live in the **ocean**.

old

1. Someone who is **old** has lived for a long time.

2. Something **old** has been used a lot.

open

When something is **open**, you can go in and out of it, or get at the things inside.

orange

An **orange** is a round fruit with thick skin and sweet juice.

outside

The **outside** of something is the part that you can see without opening it.

over

1. If something is **over** something else, it is above it.

2. If we say the show is **over**, we mean it is finished.

owl

An **owl** is a bird with large, round eyes that makes hooting sounds and usually hunts at night.

pack

When you **pack**, you put things in a suitcase or box.

paint

Paint is something you use to color things.

pair

A **pair** is made up of two things that go together, such as a **pair** of shoes.

paper

Paper is something to write on or wrap things in.

party

A **party** is a lot of people who come together to have a good time.

pen

A **pen** is a tool for writing in ink.

pencil

You can use a **pencil** for writing or drawing. **Pencils** make marks that you can rub out easily with an eraser.

pet

A **pet** is an animal that you keep at home.

phone

A **phone** is something you can use for talking to someone who is far away from you. The word **phone** is short for "telephone."

picture

A **picture** shows what something looks like.

pie

A **pie** is a pastry crust with a filling inside. **Pies** can have fruit, meat, or other foods in them.

pig

A **pig** is a short, heavy animal kept on a farm.

plant

A **plant** is a living thing that grows in the earth or in water.

play

1. When you **play**, you do something just for fun.

2. If you **play** a piano, you make music with it.

pocket

A **pocket** is a little bag sewn on or into your clothes.

potato

A **potato** is a round vegetable that grows underground.

pour

If you **pour** something, such as water, you make it flow from one place to another.

present

A **present** is something special that you give to someone.

pretend

When you **pretend**, you make believe something is real. *Let's **pretend** to be cowboys.*

pretty

Something **pretty** is nice to look at or listen to.

Pp

prize

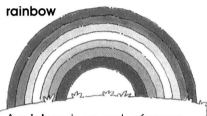

A **prize** is something won or earned in a contest or game.

promise

If you **promise** to do something, you mean you will do it.

pull

If you **pull** something, you grab it and move it toward you.

puppy

A **puppy** is a baby dog.

push

If you **push** something, you press on it to move it away from you.

puzzle

A **puzzle** is something that you have to think about in order to figure out. It can be a game, such as a crossword **puzzle** or a picture **puzzle**.

Qq

question

What is the time?

Someone who asks a **question** is trying to find something out.

quick

Someone or something that is **quick** is very fast.

quiet

If you are **quiet**, you do not make any noise.

Rr

rabbit

A **rabbit** is a small, furry animal with long ears and a small tail.

race

A **race** is a way to find out who goes the fastest.

radio

A **radio** can pick up sounds from the air. You can turn on a **radio** and listen to voices and music.

Rr

rain

Rain is water that drops from clouds in the sky.

rainbow

A **rainbow** is an arch of seven different colors.

read

When you can **read**, you can look at words and know what they mean.

ready

When you are **ready**, you have all the things you need to do something.

rest

When you **rest**, you stop what you are doing and sit or lie down for a while.

right

1. Most people draw with their **right** hand.

2. If something is **right**, it does not have any mistakes in it.

Rr

ring

1. A **ring** is something round that you wear on your finger.

2. A **ring** is also a clear sound, such as a bell makes.

river

A **river** is water that flows across the land.

road

A **road** is a way to get from place to place. Cars and buses go on **roads**.

roof

A **roof** is the cover on top of a house or other building.

run

When you **run**, you move on your feet as fast as you can.

Ss

sad

When you are **sad**, you are unhappy about something.

same

If two things are the **same**, they are alike.

school

A **school** is a place where you go to learn things.

scissors

A pair of **scissors** is something you can use to cut things, such as paper and cloth.

see
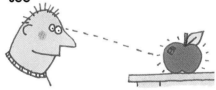

When you **see**, you look at something with your eyes.

seed

A **seed** is a small part of a plant. Most new plants grow from **seeds**.

sell

If someone **sells** you something, they give it to you in exchange for money.

sheep

A **sheep** is a four-legged animal. **Sheep** have thick wool coats.

shout

A **shout** is a loud cry you make when you want somebody to hear you.

show

1. When you **show** something, you let people see it.

2. A **show** is something you can watch at a theater or circus. You can also watch **shows** on TV.

shut

If you **shut** something, such as an open door, you close it.

sick

If you are **sick**, you do not feel well.

sign

A **sign** is a mark or words that tell you something.

Ss

sing

When you **sing**, you use your voice to make music.

sky

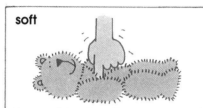

The **sky** is the space above you when you are outdoors.

sleep

When you **sleep**, you rest with your eyes closed. You don't know what is going on around you.

slow

People, animals, and things that are **slow** don't move very fast.

small

Creatures or things that are **small** are little in size. *Ants and worms are small.*

smell

When you **smell** something, you're aware of it through your nose.

smile

A **smile** is a happy look. When you **smile**, the corners of your mouth go up.

snow

Snow is frozen rain. **Snow** falls from the sky in little pieces called snowflakes.

soap

Soap is something that you use with water to help make things clean.

soft

If something is **soft**, you can push your fingers into it easily.

sound

A **sound** is anything that you can hear.

spoon

A **spoon** is something you use to eat food with. It has a small, shallow bowl at its end.

spring

Spring is the time of year between winter and summer.

stairs

Stairs are steps for walking up and down.

star

A **star** looks like a tiny light in the sky at night.

start

When you **start** doing something, you begin to do it.

stop

If you **stop** doing something, you don't do it for a while.

story

A **story** tells about things that have happened. A **story** can be about real things, or it can be made up.

summer

Summer is the time of year between spring and fall.

sun

The **sun** is the nearest star to Earth. The **sun** gives us light and keeps us warm.

swim

When you **swim**, you move in the water and stay afloat by using your arms and legs.

Tt

table

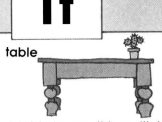

A **table** is something with legs and a flat top to put things on.

talk

When you **talk**, you say words out loud.

taste

You **taste** things when you put them in your mouth.

teach

When someone **teaches** you, they help you learn how to do something.

teeth

Teeth are the hard, white things in your mouth. You use your **teeth** to bite and chew your food.

throw

When you **throw** something, you send it through the air.

tiger

A **tiger** is a big cat that often has orange fur with black stripes.

top

The **top** is the highest part of something.

towel

A **towel** is something you use to dry yourself or other things.

town

A **town** is a place where there are houses and other buildings. People live and work in **towns**.

toy

A **toy** is something that you can play with.

train

A **train** is a lot of railroad cars together in a line. An engine pulls the **train** along a track.

tree

A **tree** is a tall plant. The main part of a **tree** is called a trunk.

truck

A **truck** is a machine made to carry big or heavy things.

TV

A **TV** picks up pictures and sounds from the air. **TV** is short for "television."

Uu

ugly

Things that are **ugly** are not nice to look at.

umbrella

An **umbrella** is something you hold over your head to keep the rain or the sun off of you.

under

If something is **under** you, it is lower than you are.

Vv

valley

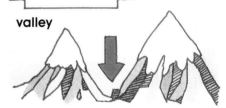

A **valley** is the low land between hills or mountains.

vegetable

A **vegetable** is a plant that you can eat. Carrots, onions, and potatoes are **vegetables**.

visit

If someone **visits** you, they come to see you.

walk

When you **walk**, you move along on your feet without running.

warm

When you are **warm**, you are not cold.

wash

When you **wash** something, you make it clean by using soap and water.

watch

1. When you **watch** something, you look at it for some time.

2. A **watch** is a small clock that you can wear.

water

Water is something you drink and wash with. It also falls from the sky as rain and fills rivers, lakes, and oceans.

weather

The **weather** is what it is like outdoors. You wear a coat if the **weather** is cold.

week

A **week** is seven days. There are fifty-two **weeks** in a year.

wet

If something is **wet**, it is covered or soaked with liquid.

wind

Wind is quickly moving air. A gentle **wind** is called a breeze.

window

A **window** is a place where light and air can come in. **Windows** usually have glass in them.

wing

The **wings** of a bird, a bat, or an insect are the parts of its body that it uses to fly. Airplanes have **wings**, too.

winter

Winter is the time of the year between fall and spring.

woman

A **woman** is an adult female person. A girl grows up to be a **woman**.

word

Words are the things you use when you speak or write.

write

To **write** is to put words on something such as paper.

x ray

An **x ray** is a picture doctors use to see if any bones are broken. An **x ray** shows the inside of something.

yawn

When you **yawn**, you open your mouth very wide and breathe in and out. You sometimes **yawn** if you are sleepy.

year

A **year** is the same as 12 months, or 52 weeks, or 365 days.

young

Someone who is **young** has not been alive very long.

zipper

A **zipper** is something that is used to hold things together. Some clothes and bags have **zippers** on them.

zoo

A **zoo** is a safe place for people to see wild animals and learn more about them.

It seems nearly everybody is in a rush to get to **WORD FUN!** Just turn the page...

Word Fun

What Doesn't Belong Here?

Using a pencil and a blank piece of paper, write down the words that go with these pictures. Circle the word, *not* the picture, that doesn't belong in each group.

1.

2.

3.

The Long and Short of It

The longest words in the A-to-Z section of this book have nine letters each. Can you find all four of those words? Only one word in the A-to-Z section of this book has two letters. Can you find that word? Write all your answers down on a piece of paper.

Word Fun

Silly Riddles

Can you come up with a one-word answer that fits each silly riddle here?
Write each word down on a piece of paper.

1. What's the loudest part of a tree?
2. If you suddenly drop to the ground, what time of the year is it?
3. What small, furry, winged animal is also used in some games?

Have You Met Your Match?

Here's a matching contest that will show just how many words you've learned.
Take a blank piece of paper and write the numbers 1 through 10 from top to
bottom on the left-hand side. Next to each of the numbers you've written down,
write the word from Column B that best fits the picture or phrase found in
Column A. Good luck!

Column A

1.

2. tool for writing in ink

3.

4. the food you eat first thing in the morning

5.

6. someone you like very much

7.

8. a baby cat

9.

10. something to wear on your head

Column B

hat
dog
balloon
radio
clock
ring
pen
breakfast
kitten
friend

Word Fun

The Lost Ring

You've already shown how well you can "read a picture." But can you also crack a secret message? Every time you see a picture in this story, write down the word it goes with on a blank piece of paper. After that, write down only the first letter of each of those *pictured* words. Those letters spell a secret message.

Molly was happy. There was a  high in the

sky as she played. Her 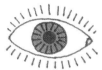 could also see an

 far off in the distance. What a good day she

was having!

But then, she saw that her ring was missing from her finger. "Oh, no!" she cried. "Where could it be?"

At that moment, a  came by, dug a hole,

snatched a bone out of it, and ran off. Thinking the dog may have taken and buried her ring, Molly looked into the hole for it. But the ring wasn't there.

Molly now searched the ground on her hands and

knees, scaring off some  .

Word Fun

Then she looked into a  on a low tree branch.

After that, she walked through a

and looked  a flower. Some  from

the flower stuck to her clothes.

Suddenly, Molly tripped over a rock, surprising a

 behind it. When she hit the ground,

something shook loose from her pocket.

Standing up, Molly saw that it was her ring. It had been in her pocket the whole time! "Now I remember!" said Molly. "I put the ring in my pocket when I washed my hands before going out to play."

Thunder cracked overhead. "I better get home before

it rains again," she said. "I forgot to bring my  ."

Slipping the ring on her finger, Molly sniffed the air.

Her  caught the smell of dinner cooking. So

she ran home.

Word Fun

ANSWERS

What Doesn't Belong Here?
1. bus, car, watch, truck; *watch* doesn't belong here.
2. fork, knife, pie, spoon; *pie* doesn't belong here.
3. bear, elephant, fish, tiger; *fish* doesn't belong here.

The Long and Short of It
The longest words in the A-to-Z section of the book are *butterfly, different, important,* and *vegetable.* The shortest word is *TV.*

Silly Riddles
1. its *bark;* 2. *fall;* 3. a *bat*

Have You Met Your Match?
1. clock; 2. pen; 3. balloon; 4. breakfast; 5. dog; 6. friend; 7. ring; 8. kitten; 9. radio; 10. hat

The Lost Ring
In order, the words are: **r**ainbow, **e**yes, **a**irplane, **d**og, **i**nsects, **n**est, **g**arden, **i**nside, **s**eeds, **f**rog, **u**mbrella, **n**ose. The first letters of all these words spell **reading is fun.**